CLASSICAL MANDOLIN SOLOS

Complied, arranged and recorded by Carlo Aonzo

To access audio visit:
www.halleonard.com/mylibrary

Enter Code
7278-9611-8201-6784

ISBN 978-1-4803-7100-2

7777 W. BLUEMOUND RD. P.O. BOX 13819 MILWAUKEE, WI 53213

In Australia Contact:
Hal Leonard Australia Pty. Ltd.
4 Lentara Court
Cheltenham, Victoria, 3192 Australia
Email: ausadmin@halleonard.com.au

Visit Hal Leonard Online at
www.halleonard.com

ABOUT THE ARRANGER

Carlo Aonzo is a native of Savona, Italy, where he grew up immersed in music from his father, Giuseppe, who instilled in him a love and respect for the mandolin. After he went on to study with Ugo Orlandi at the Cesare Pollini Conservatory in Padua, where Carlo graduated summa cum laude in 1993, his playing has been recognized with rewards at prestigious competitions, including the "Vivaldi" prize of the 6th annual Vittorio Pitzianti National Mandolin Competition in Venice and first prize at the 27th annual Walnut Valley National Contest in Winfield, Kansas. Carlo has toured throughout Europe, Japan, the USA, and Canada as a soloist and with chamber ensembles and orchestras, and has worked with many musical institutions including La Scala Philharmonic in Milan.

INTRODUCTION

The order of the pieces in this book is not chronological. Rather, it reflects my own path of musical growth. Its progression is based on the technical difficulties of each composition, ending with true complete concert pieces that require the most advanced mandolin techniques.

We start with the first exercises from Giuseppe Branzoli's mandolin method. My father, my first teacher, used these with me when I first began studying the mandolin. They are easy, but at the same time are real compositions suitable for private performance occasions for you or your students.

The sonata by Filippo Sauli is an example of early 18th-century Baroque music. This original piece, written in tablature, is meant for a mandolin tuned with intervals of a fourth. It is here adapted to the Neapolitan variety of mandolin.

The late 18th century is represented by the arias with variations by mandolinist and teacher Gabriele Leone, derived from his teaching method published in Paris. Antonio Riggieri's aria with variations constitutes another wonderful example of late Baroque/early Classical virtuoso technique.

Bartolomeo Bortolazzi is the most important composer for mandolin in the Classical era. Since there is no solo piece by this interesting virtuoso musician, I often use my arrangement for solo mandolin of the "Theme with Variations in A major," originally for mandolin and guitar.

We then proceed to the late 19th century and showcase two different aspects of the mandolin repertoire: a "light" piece, a Mazurka by Rosario Gargano, and three compositions from the pen of Carlo Munier. Considered the founding father of the modern mandolin school, Munier composed one of the most famous pieces for the instrument, "Capriccio Spagnuolo." At the time it was written, due to commercial needs, the work was published in a variety of arrangements, from a single instrument up to full orchestra. We present it here in its solo mandolin version.

The collection ends with three pieces by Raffaele Calace: Prelude II, Prelude X, and the "Cielo Stellato" nocturne. These are the most representative and frequently performed pieces by this highly important mandolin composer. For a long time, his preludes were considered the summation of modern mandolin technique.

As an appendix, there is a piece from the other side of the Atlantic. "Golden Rod," a barcarolle by Valentine Abt, is an astonishing work, showing the development achieved by the classical mandolin in the New World.

I hope you will enjoy the music in this book as much as I have cherished it throughout my musical career. It offers the discovery of innumerable technical and creative possibilities hidden inside our instrument. May this be a starting point of never-ending enrichment of your personal expressivity.

—Carlo Aonzo

from the mandolin method *A Theoretical and Practical Method for the Mandolin*

Exercise in D major

Giuseppe Branzoli

from the mandolin method *A Theoretical and Practical Method for the Mandolin*

Exercise in B minor

Giuseppe Branzoli

Moderately slow

from the mandolin method *A Theoretical and Practical Method for the Mandolin*

Exercise in G minor

Giuseppe Branzoli

Moderately, in 2

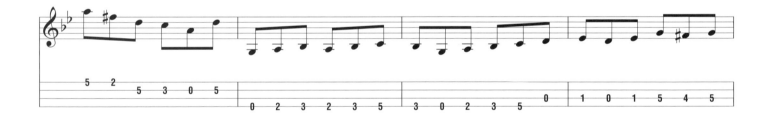

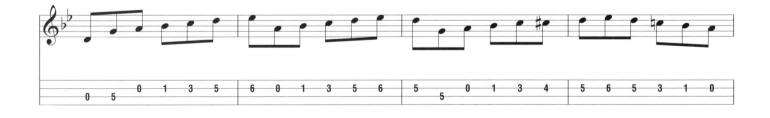

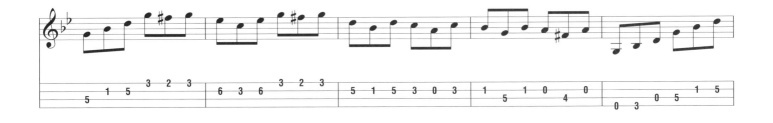

from the mandolin method *A Theoretical and Practical Method for the Mandolin*

Exercise in A major

Giuseppe Branzoli

Slow, in 1

Free time

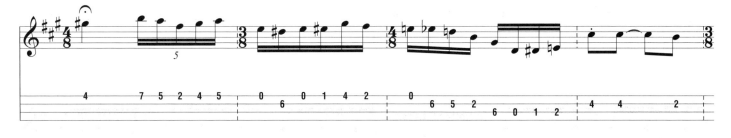

A tempo

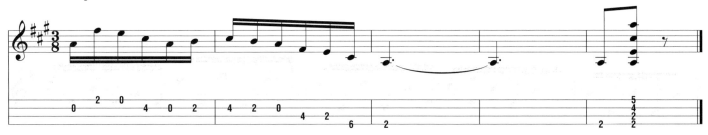

Partita V in G minor
Overture

Filippo Sauli

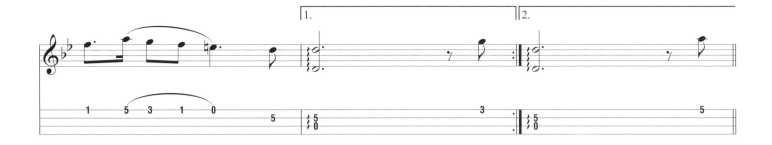

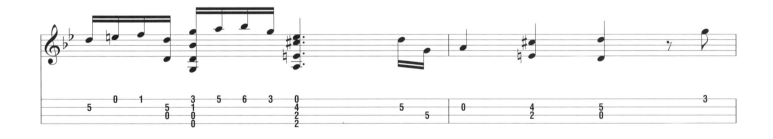

Partita V in G minor
Allemande

Filippo Sauli

Moderately slow

Partita V in G minor
Corrente

Filippo Sauli

Partita V in G minor
Sarabanda

Filippo Sauli

Moderately fast

Partita V in G minor
Giga
Filippo Sauli

Moderately fast, in 4

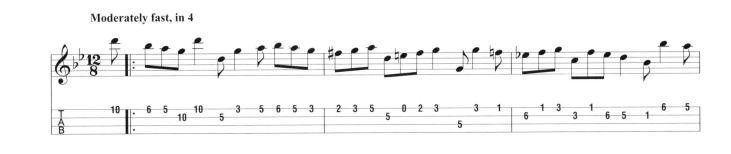

from the method *Methode Raisonné pour Passer du Violin à la Mandolin*

La lumiere la plus pure
Aria with Variations

Gabriele Leone

Variation I

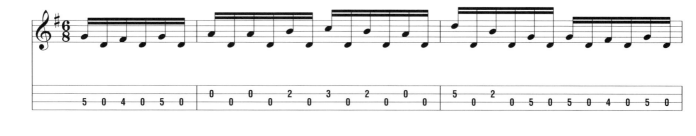

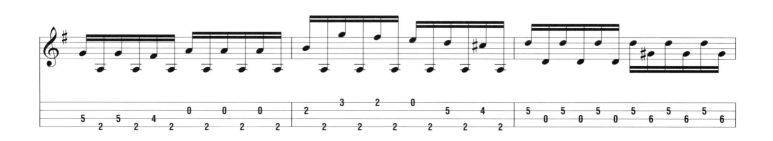

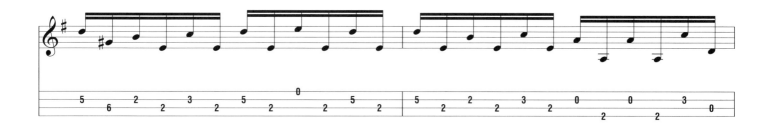

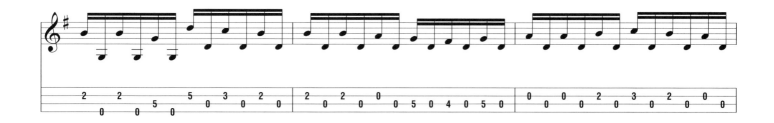

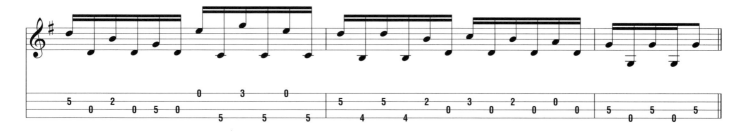

Variation II

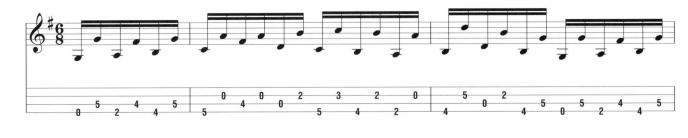

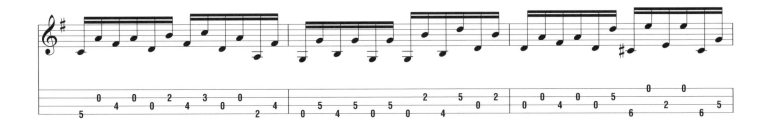

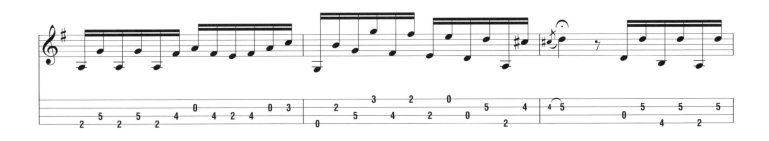

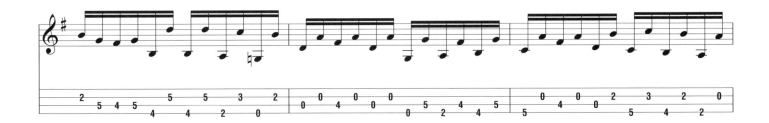

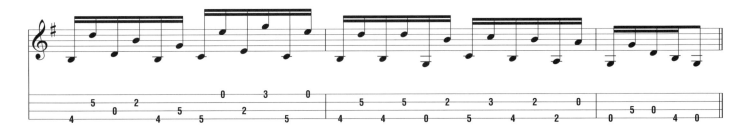

Variation III

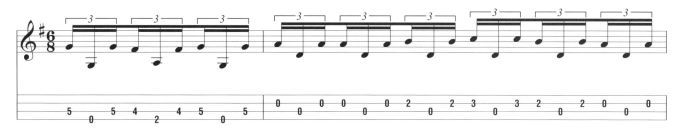

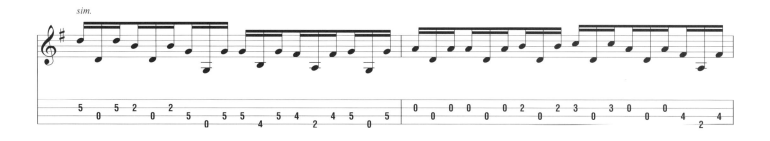

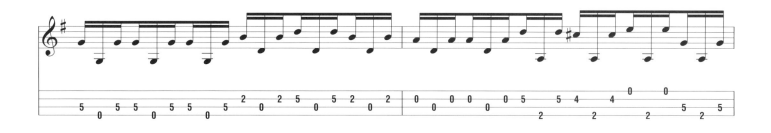

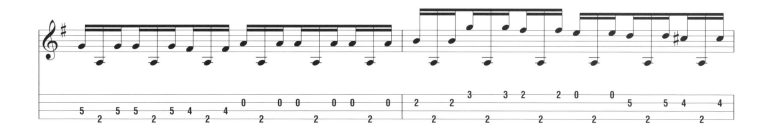

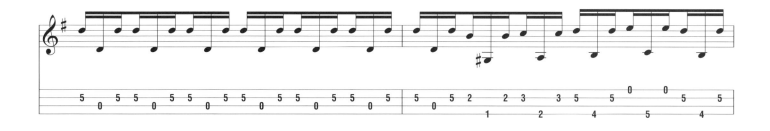

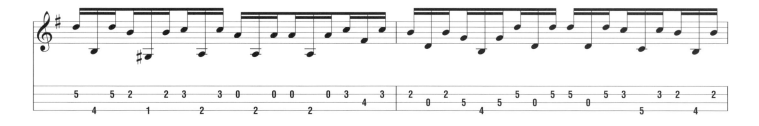

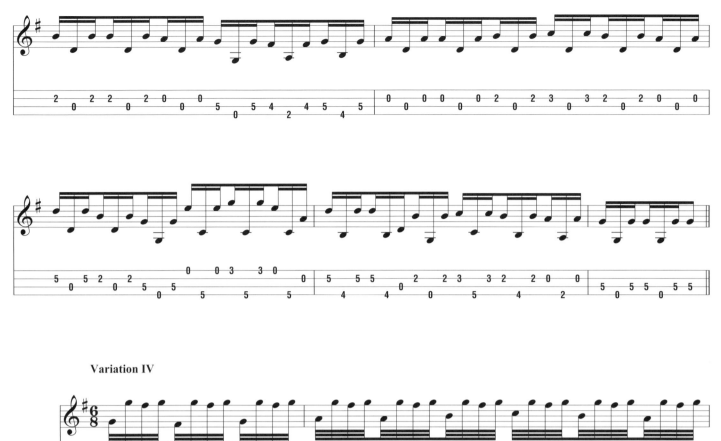

Variation IV

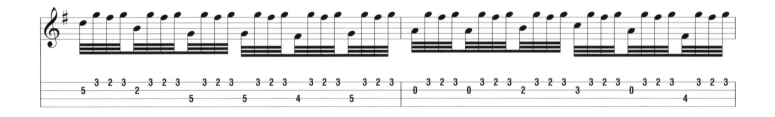

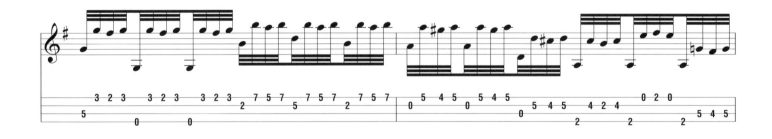

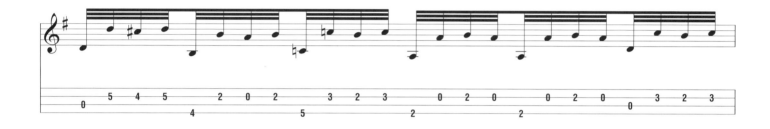

La Fustemberg
Aria with Variations

Antonio Riggieri

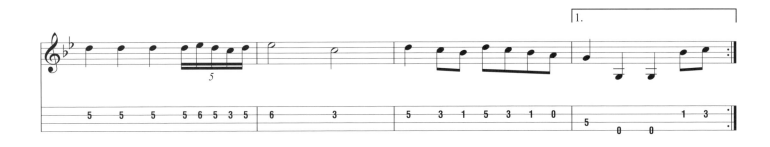

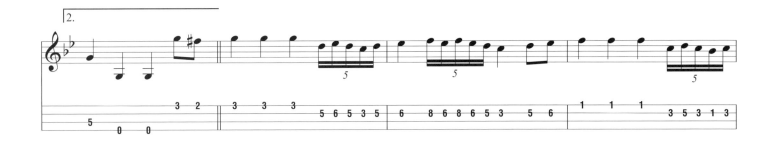

Variation I

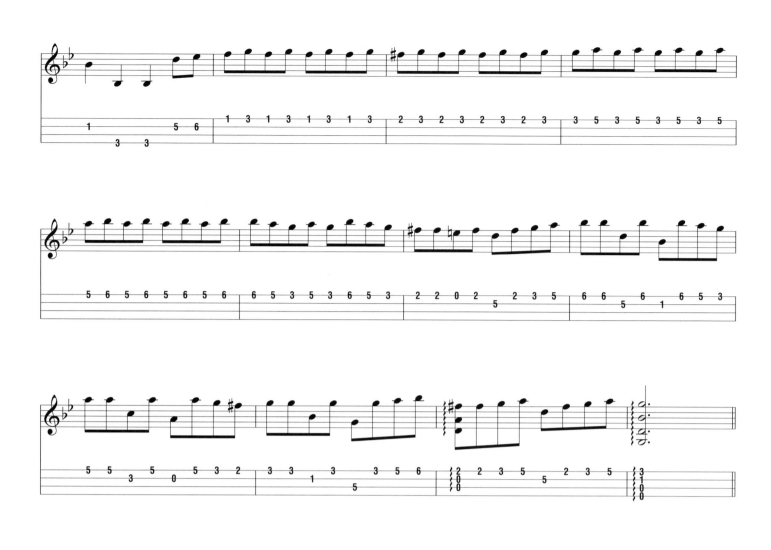

Variation II

Variation III

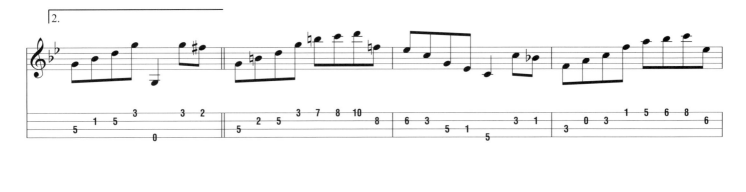

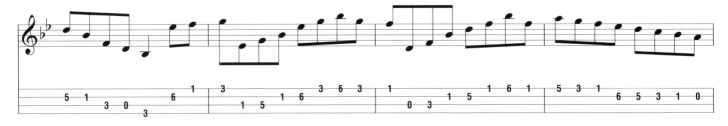

Variation IV

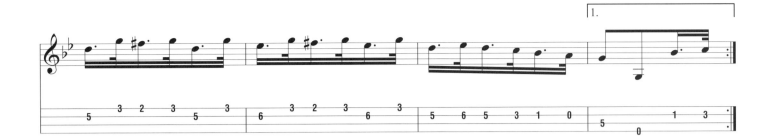

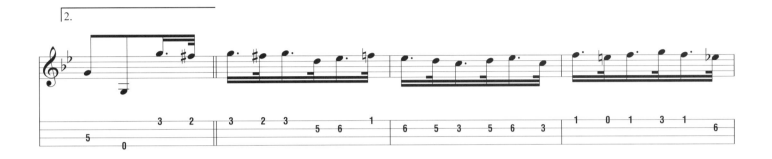

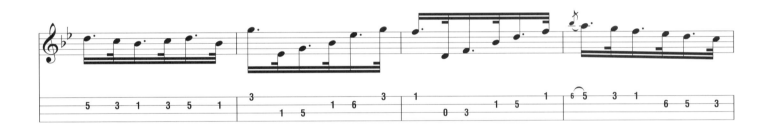

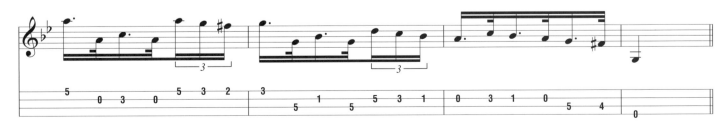

Variation V

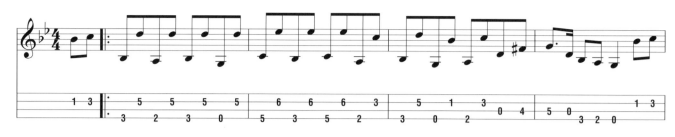

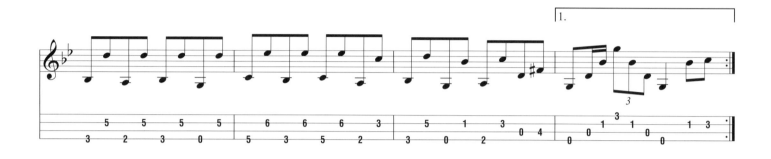

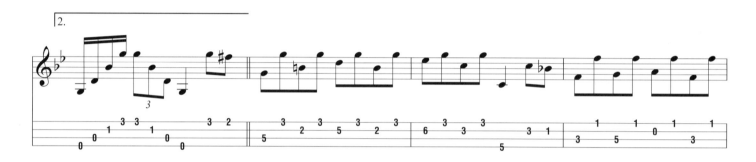

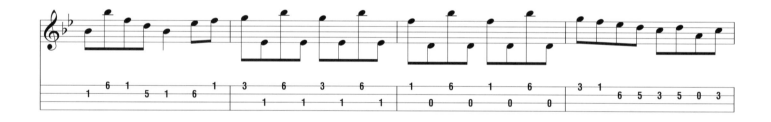

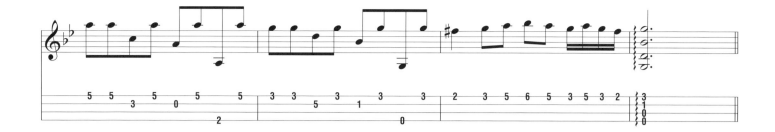

Variation VI

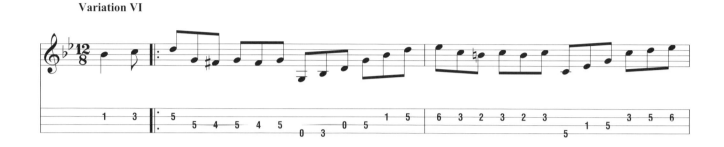

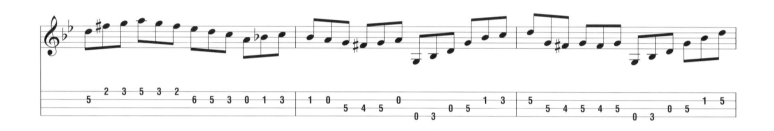

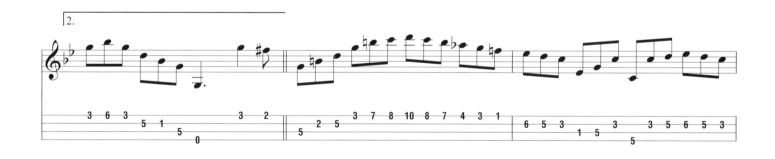

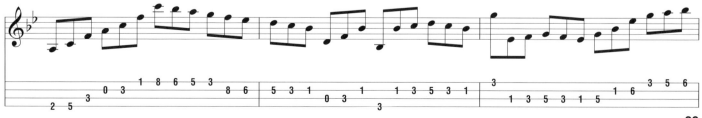

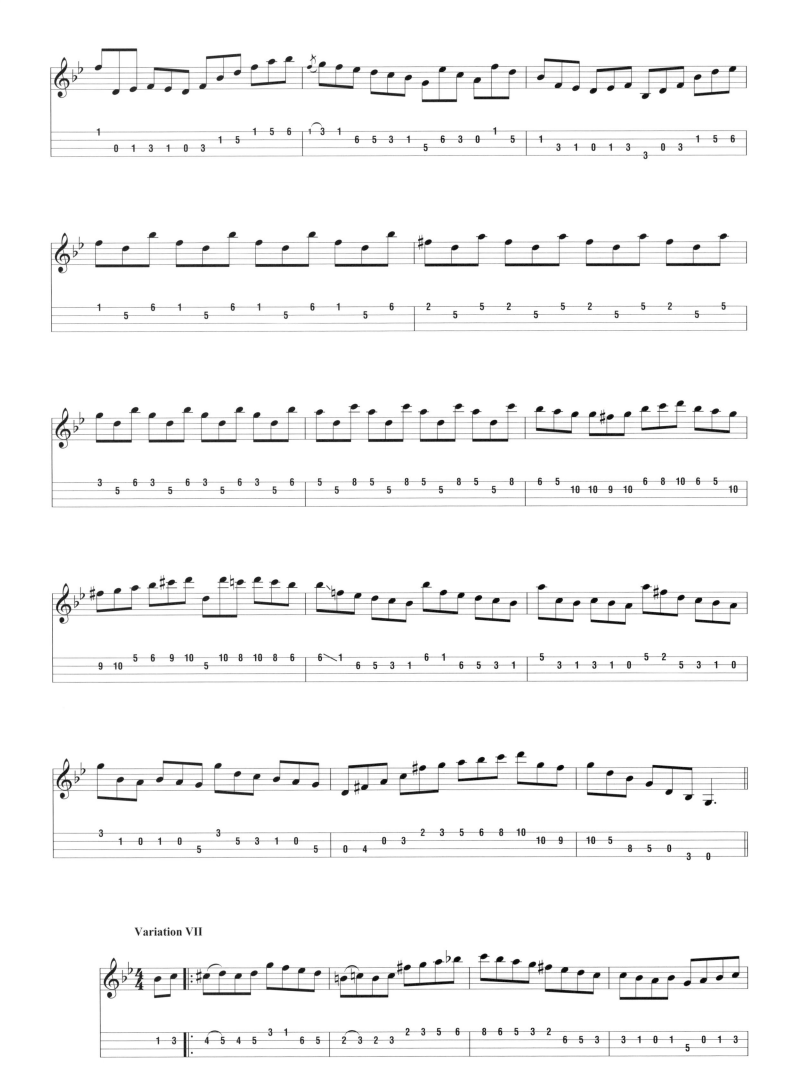

Variation VII

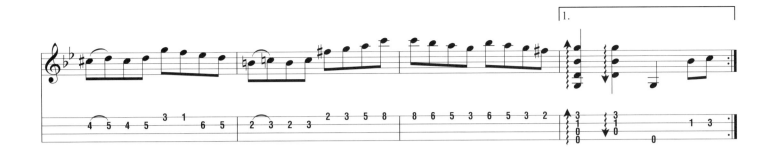

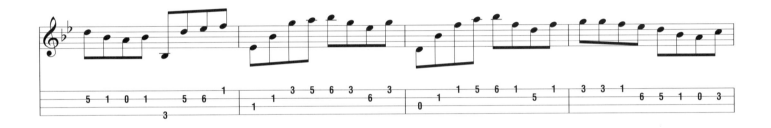

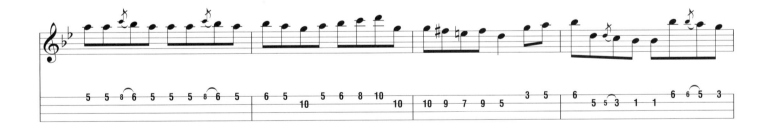

Variation VIII

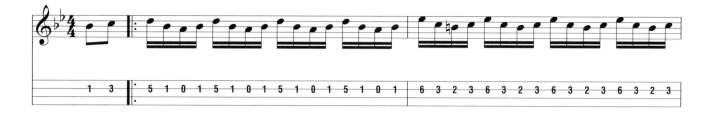

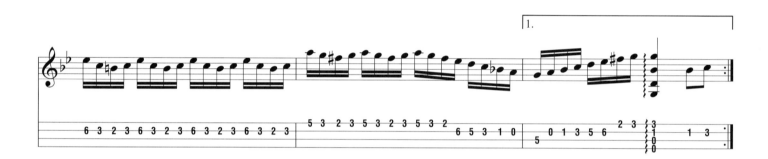

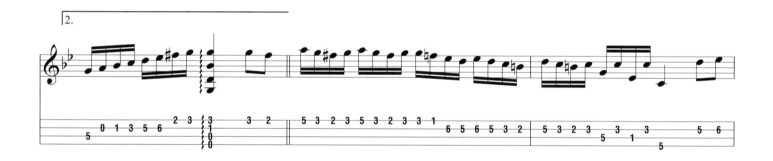

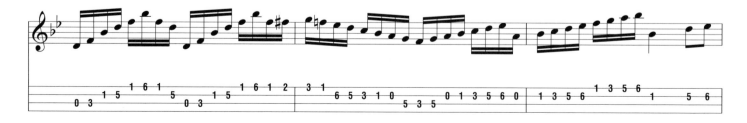

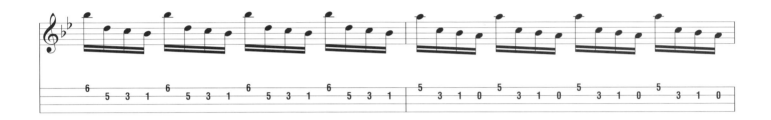

Variation IX

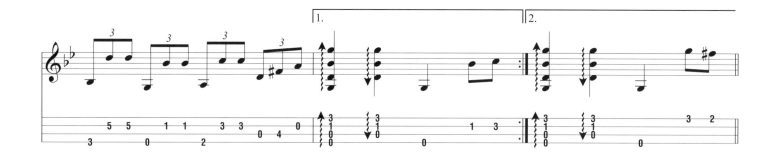

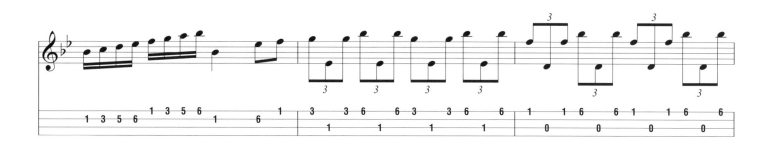

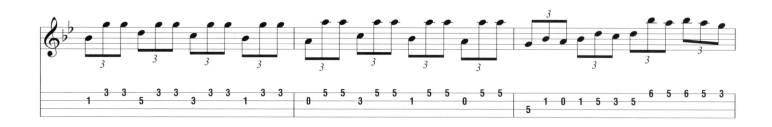

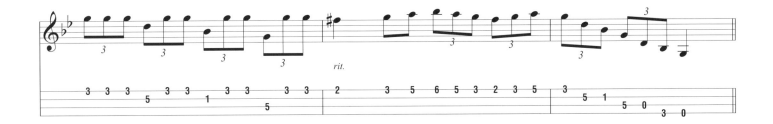

Variation X

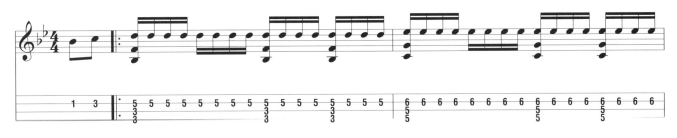

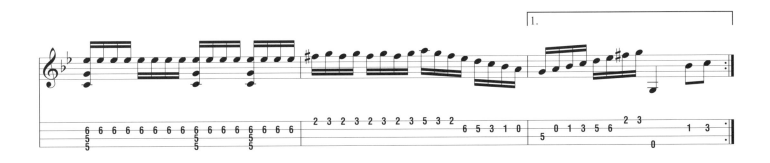

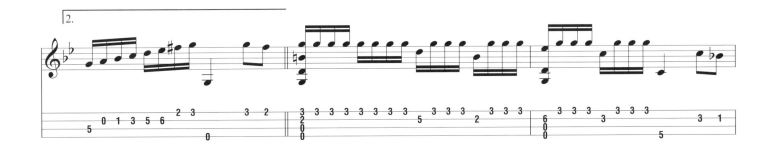

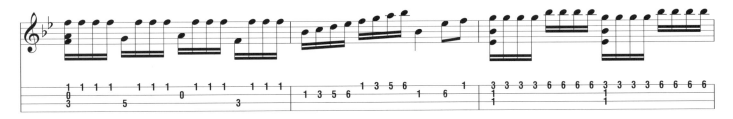

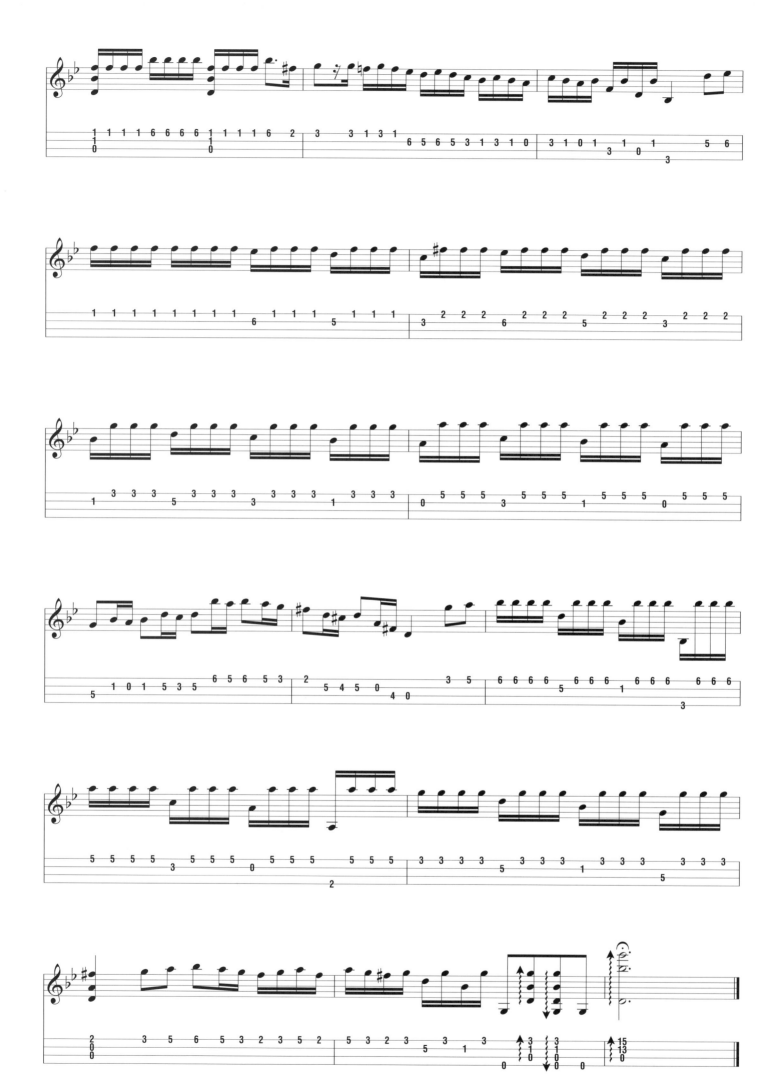

Theme with Variations in A major

Bartolomeo Bortolazzi

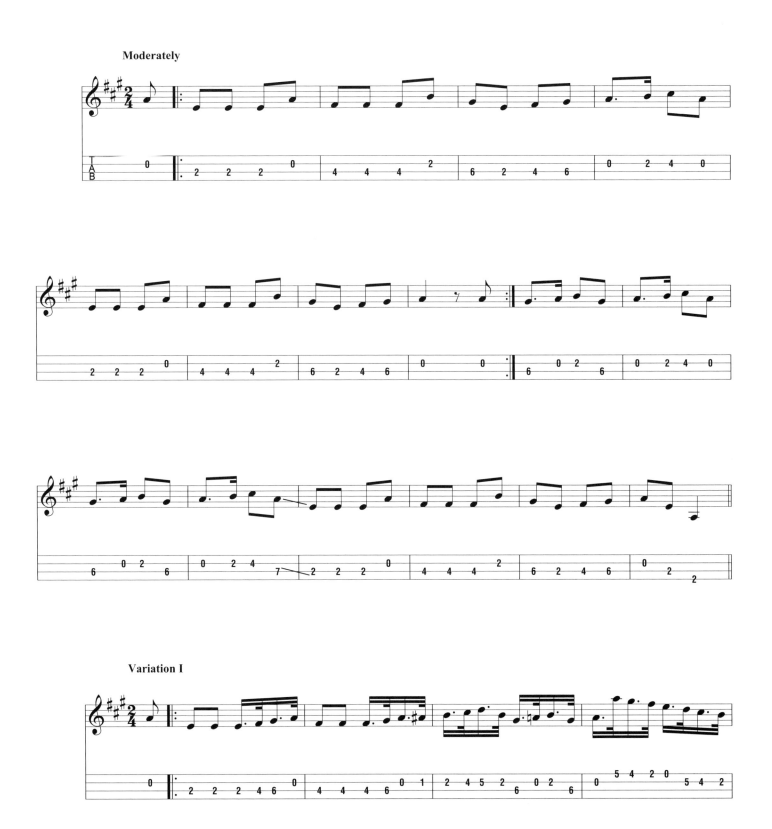

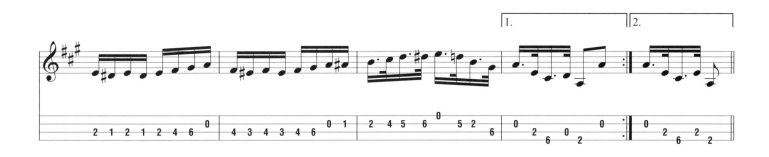

Variation II

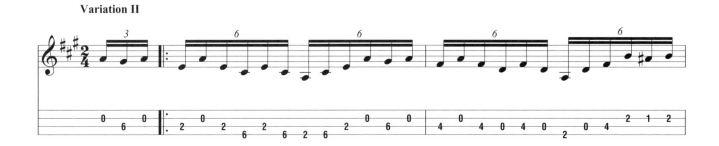

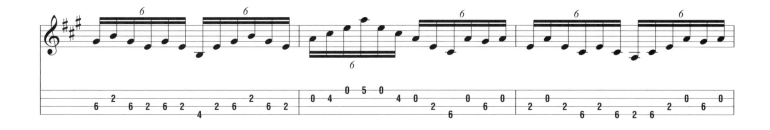

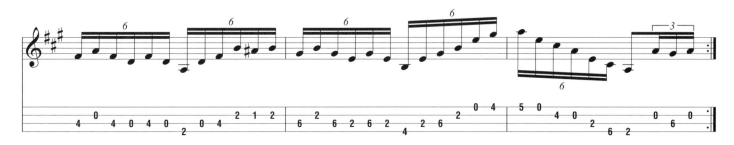

*Variation III

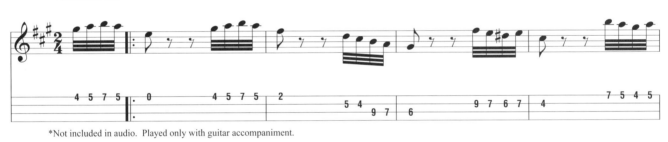

*Not included in audio. Played only with guitar accompaniment.

Variation IV

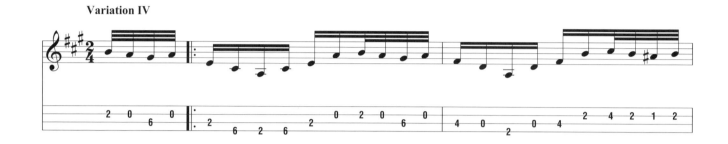

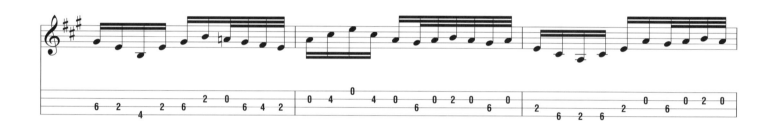

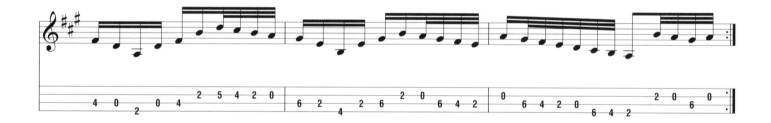

Variation V

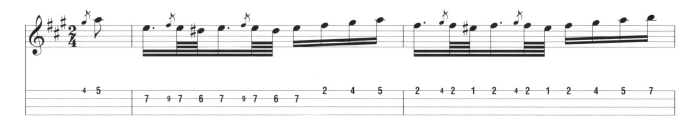

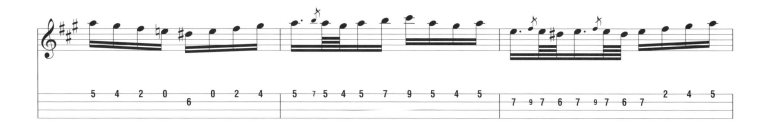

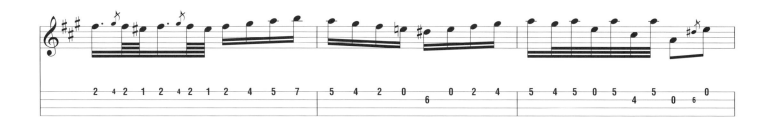

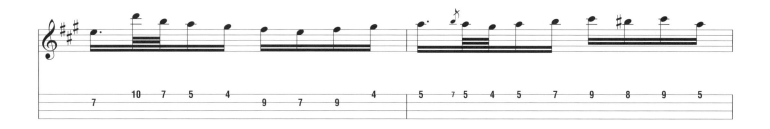

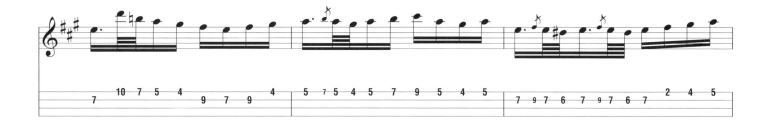

Variation VI

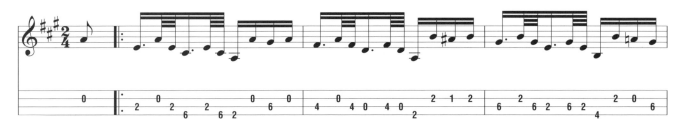

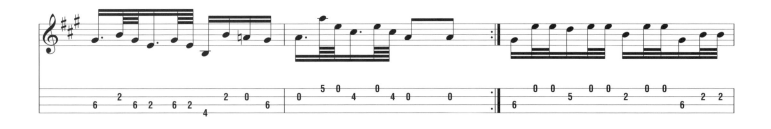

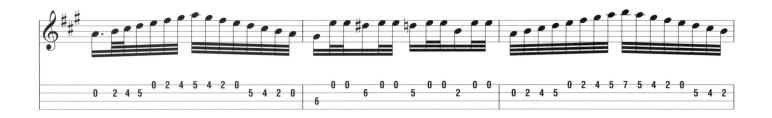

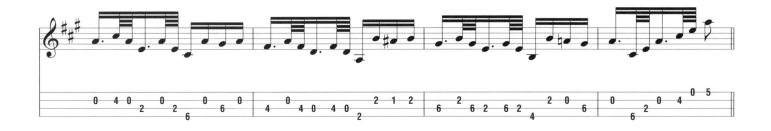

Finale
Vivace

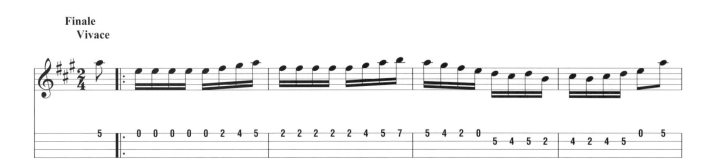

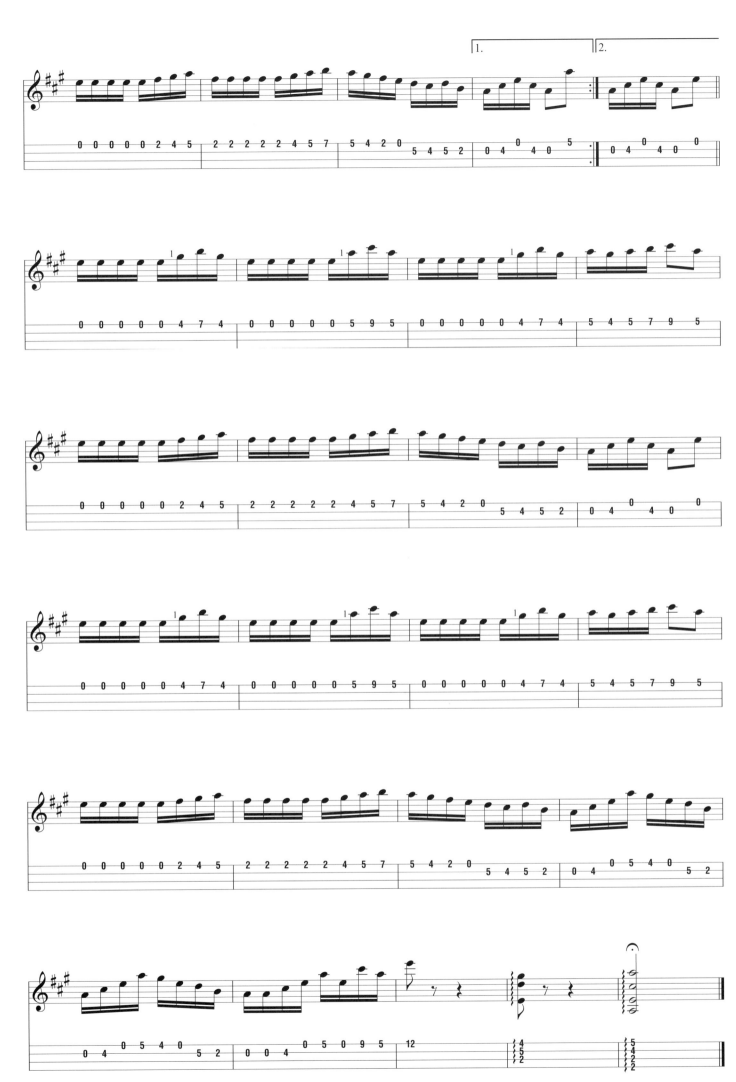

Mazurka di Concerto

Rosario Gargano

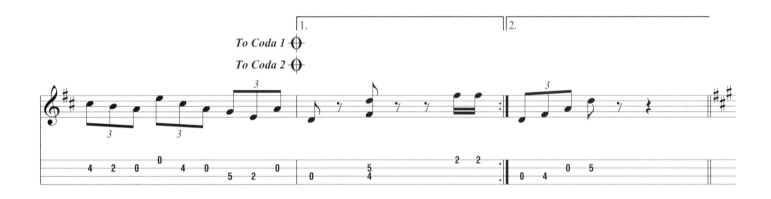

*2nd time, play top note only.

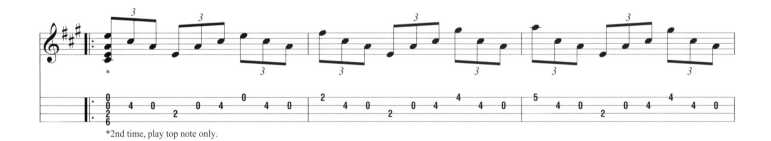

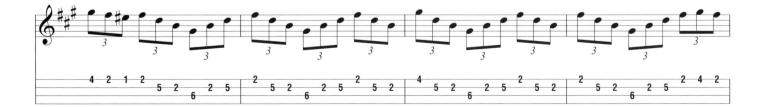

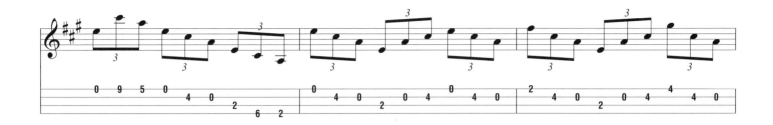

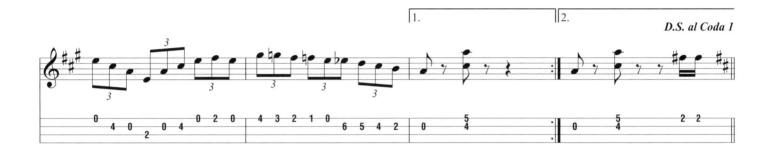

⊕ Coda 1

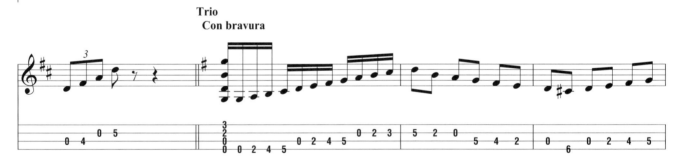

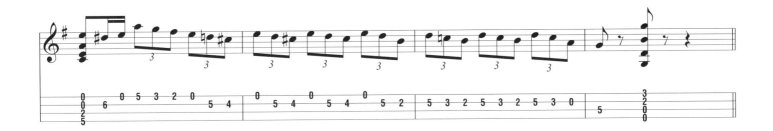

D.S. al Coda 2

⊕ **Coda 2**

Per finire

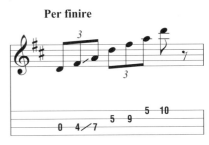

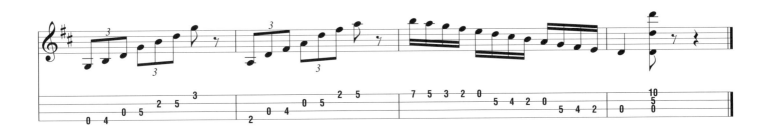

from the method *Scuola del Mandolino Metodo Pratico Completo*

Andante - Pizzicato on the Left Hand

Carlo Munier

Moderately

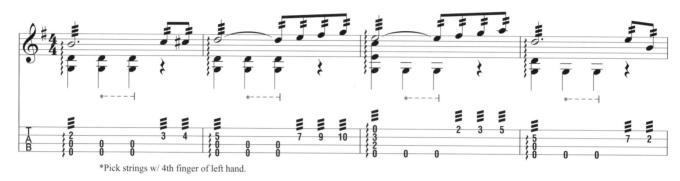

*Pick strings w/ 4th finger of left hand.

**2nd time, no trem., next 2 meas.

***Pick string w/ 3rd
finger of left hand.

†Pick string w/ 2nd
finger of left hand.

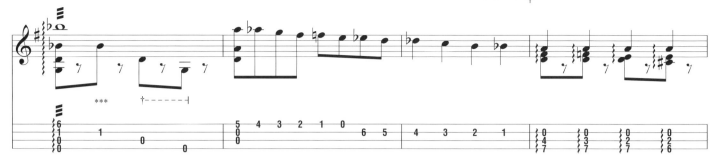

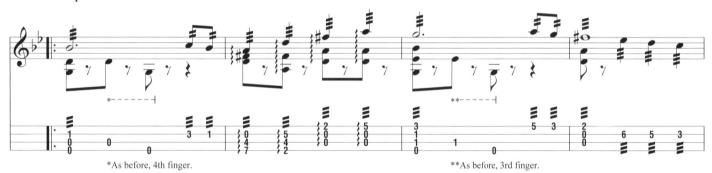

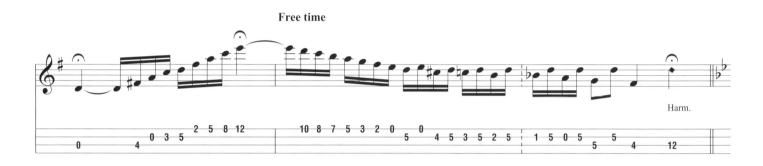

*As before, 4th finger.   **As before, 3rd finger.

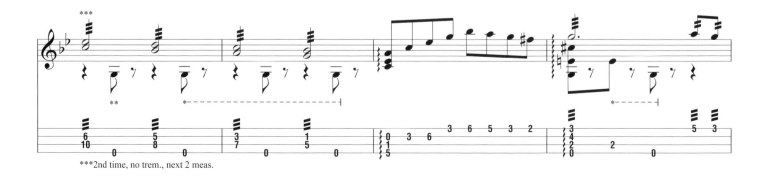

***2nd time, no trem., next 2 meas.

Coda

A tempo

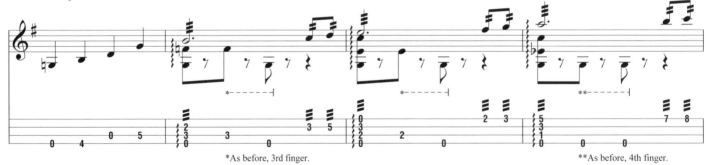

*As before, 3rd finger.

**As before, 4th finger.

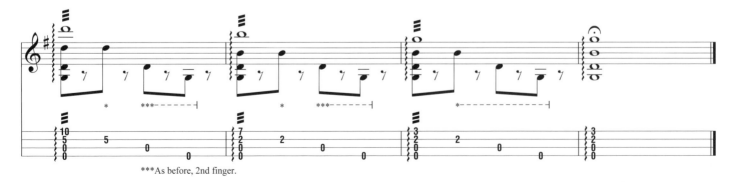

***As before, 2nd finger.

This page has been intentionally left blank
to avoid unnecessary page turns.

Love Song

Carlo Munier
Op. 275

Slow

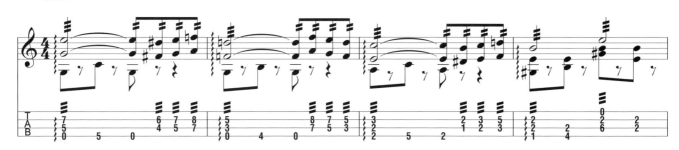

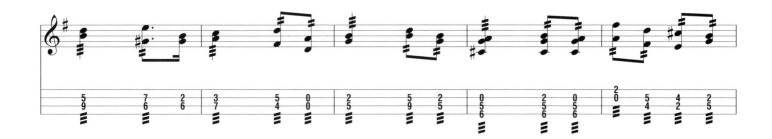

Andantino

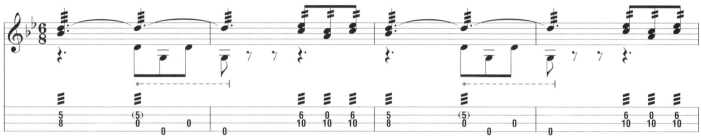

*Pick string w/ 3rd finger of left hand.

Allegretto

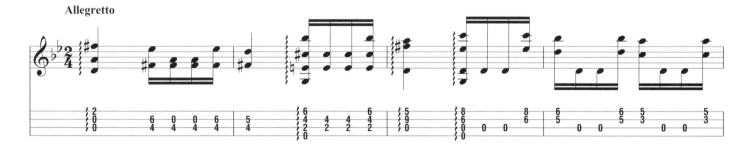

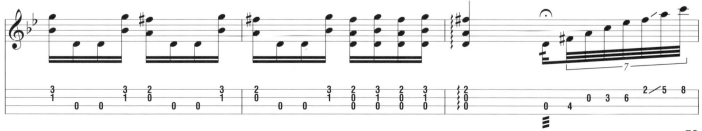

Andantino

*As before

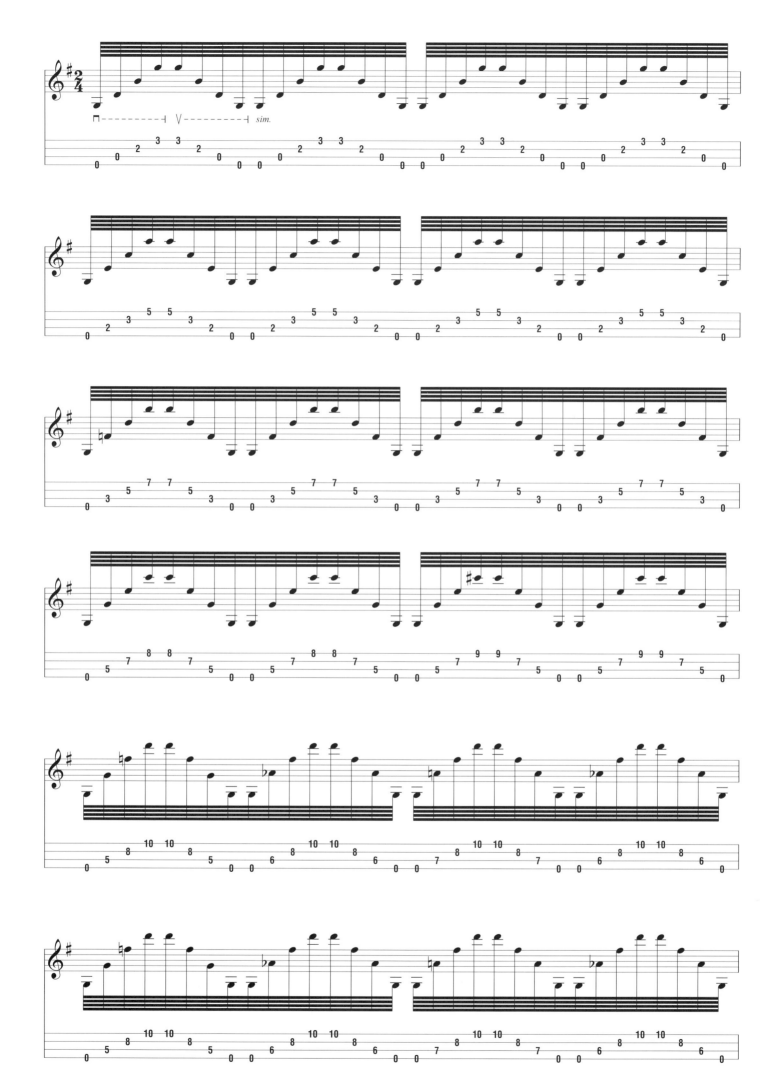

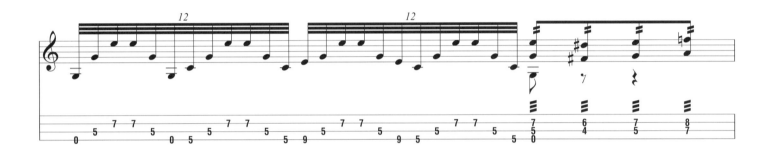

*Pick string w/ 4th finger of left hand.

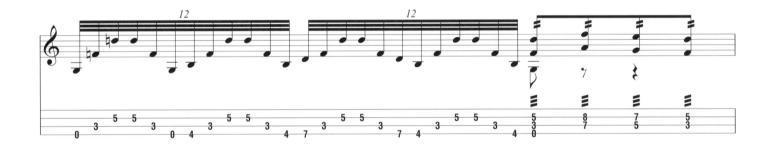

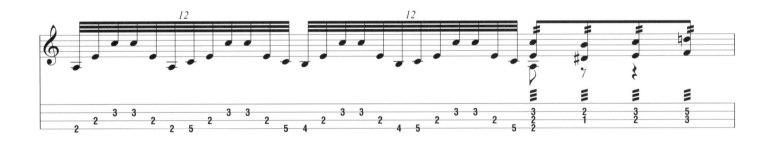

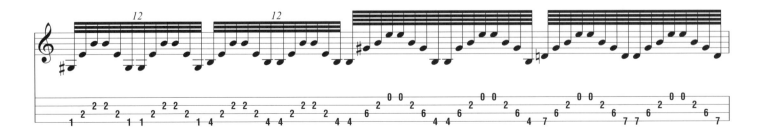

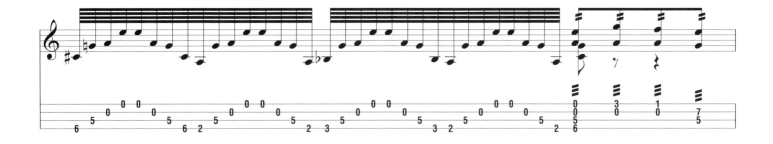

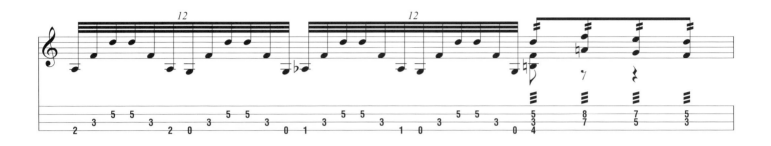

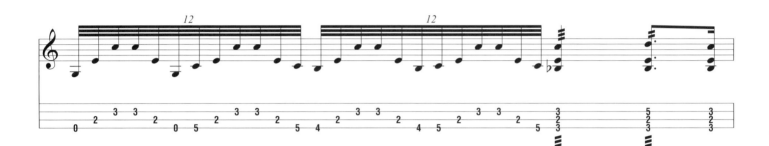

Capriccio Spagnuolo

Carlo Munier
Op. 276

To Coda

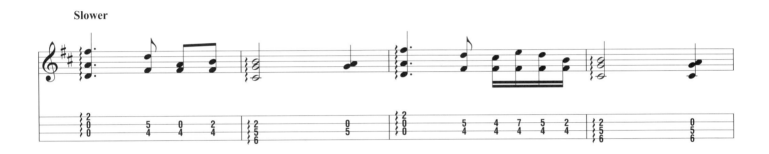

Slower

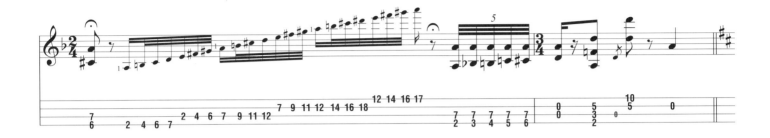

Moderately fast

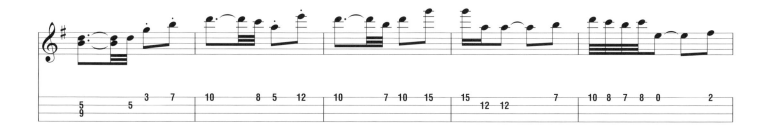

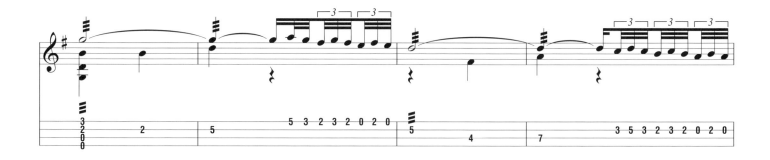

Lively

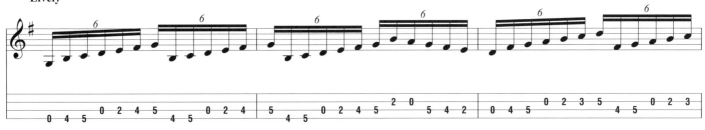

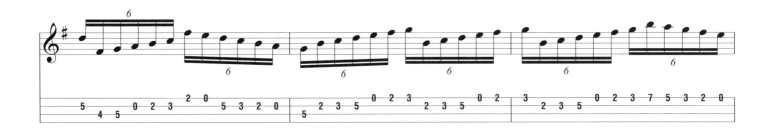

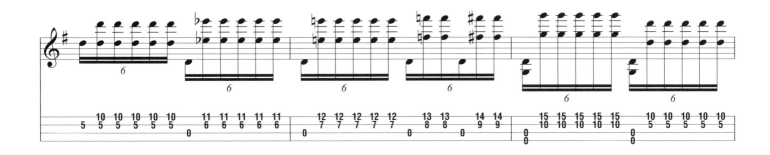

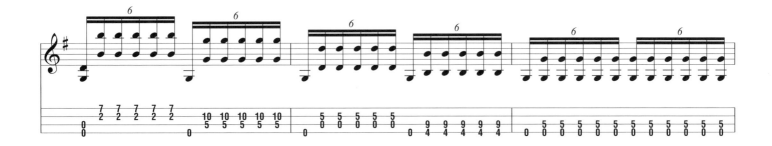

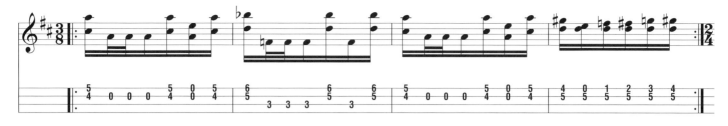

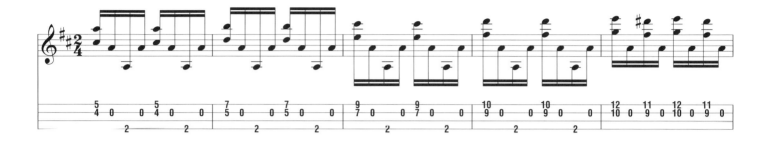

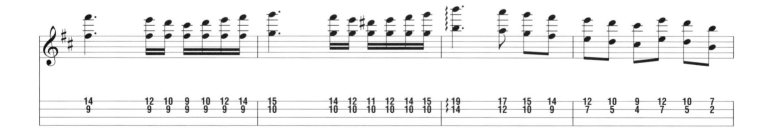

Slower

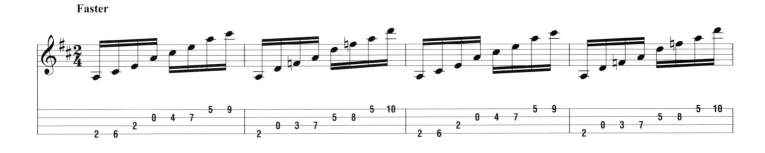

*Omitted on audio.

Faster

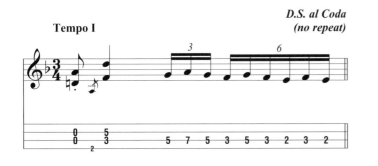

D.S. al Coda
(no repeat)

𝄌 **Coda**

Tempo I

64

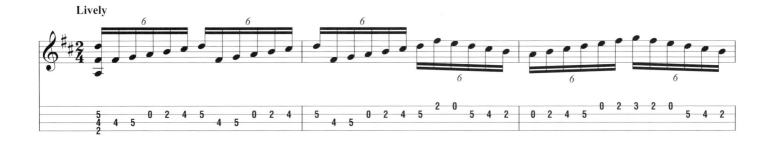

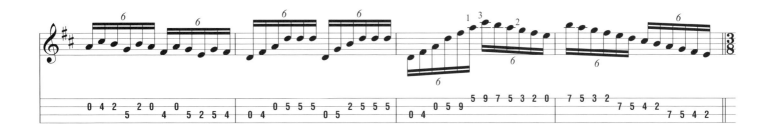

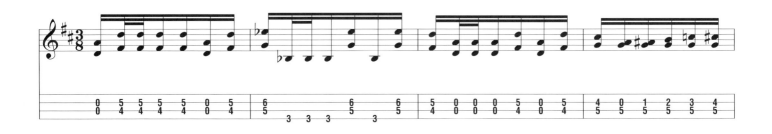

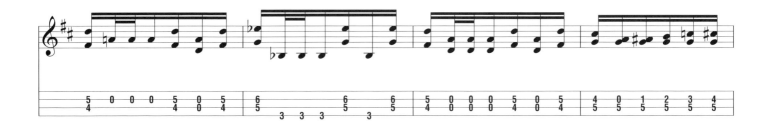

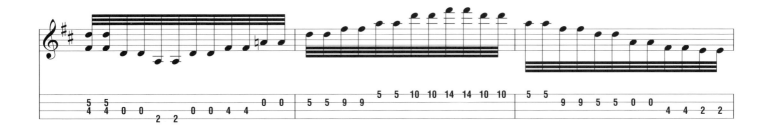

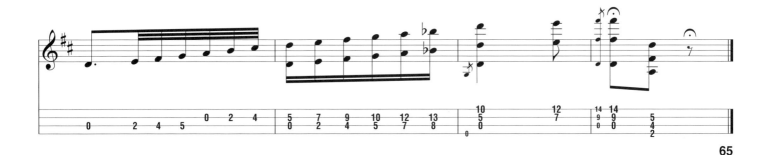

Notturno-Cielo Stellato

Raffaele Calace
Op. 186

Moderately

*Pick string w/ left hand finger.

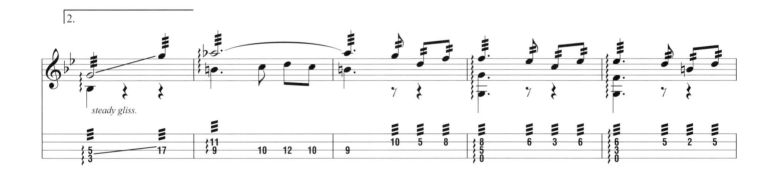

steady gliss.

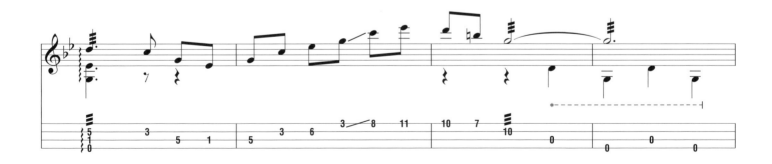

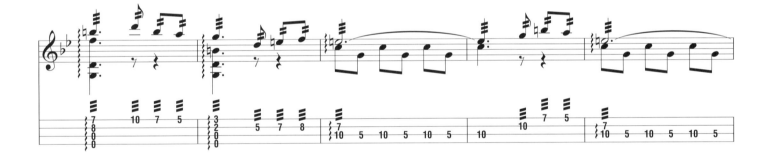

Scherzo

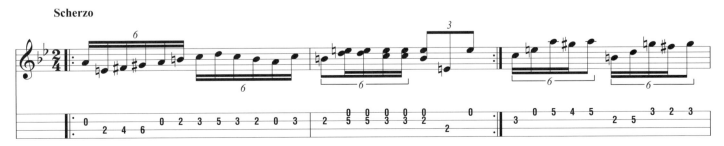

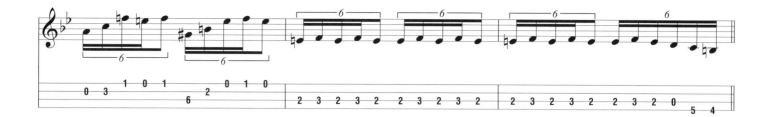

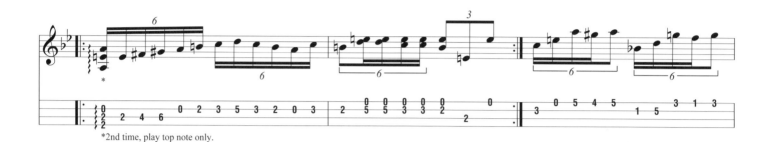

*2nd time, play top note only.

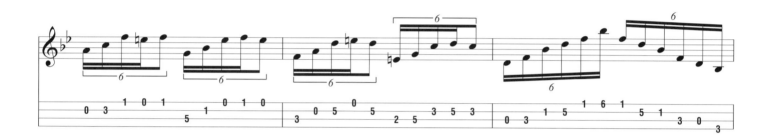

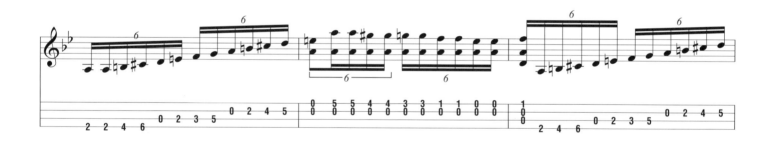

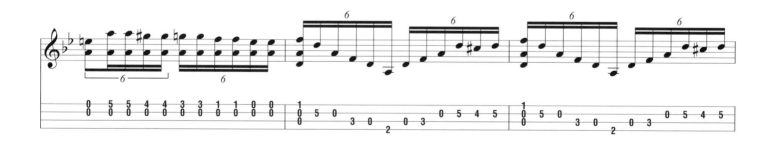

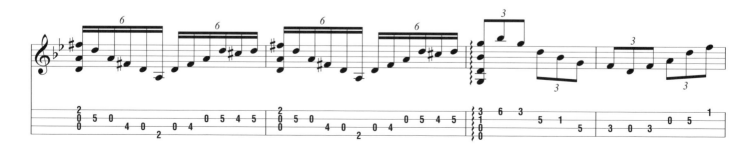

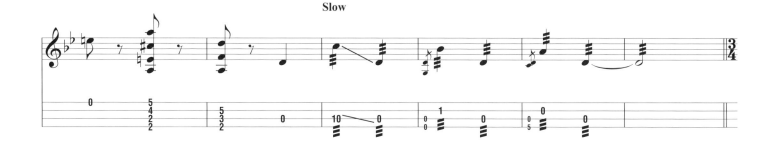

Slow

*Pick string w/ left hand finger.

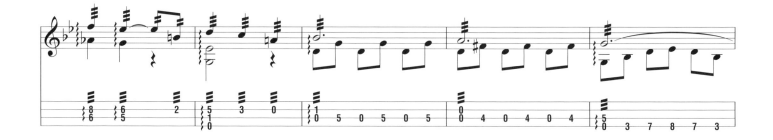

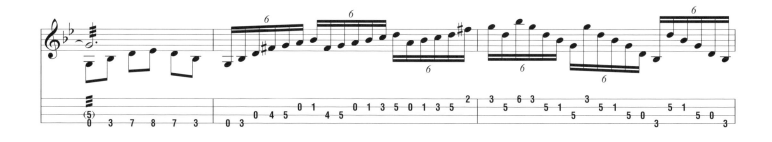

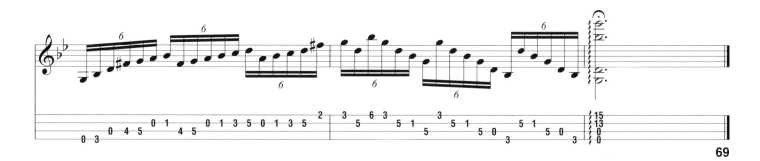

Preludio II

Raffaele Calace
Op. 49

Moderately slow

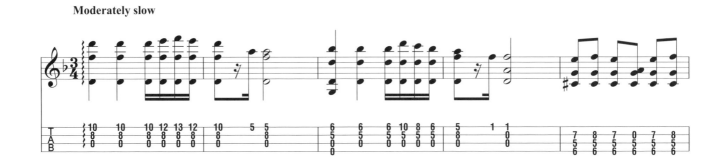

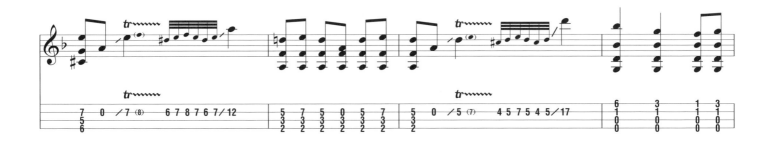

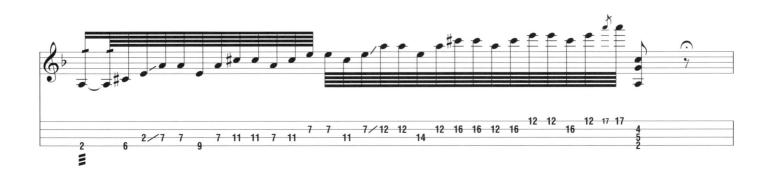

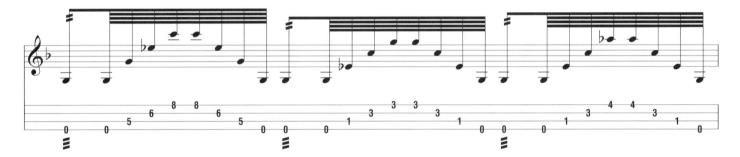

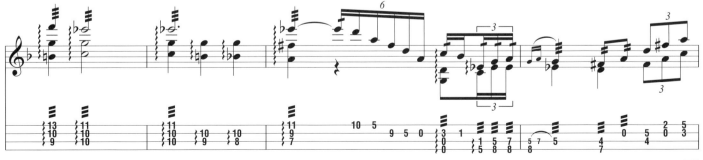

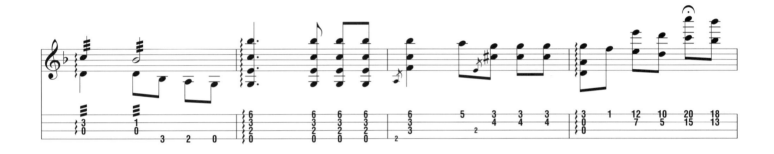

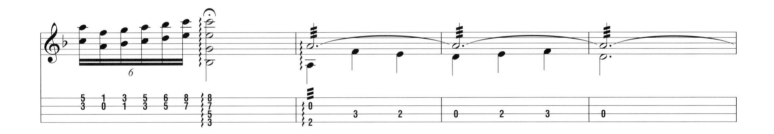

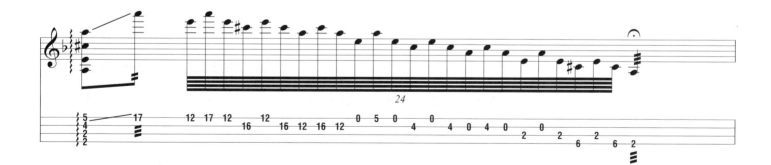

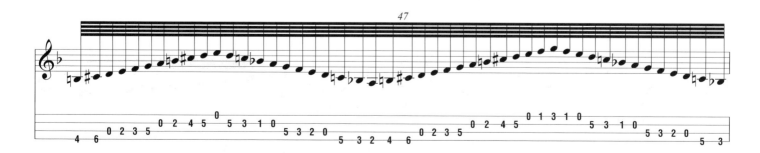

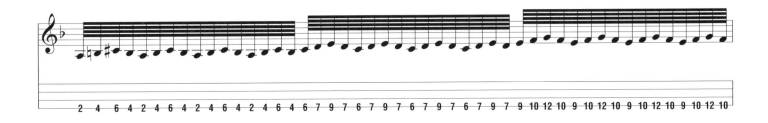

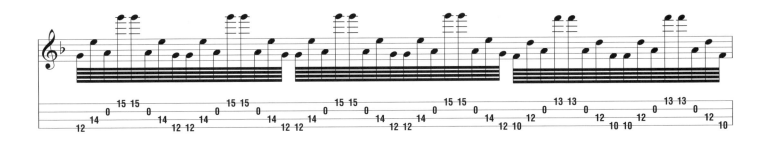

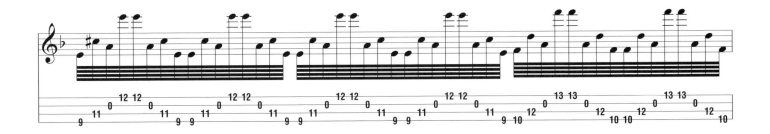

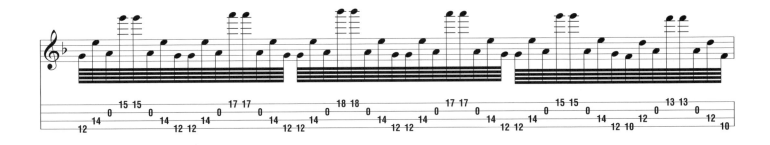

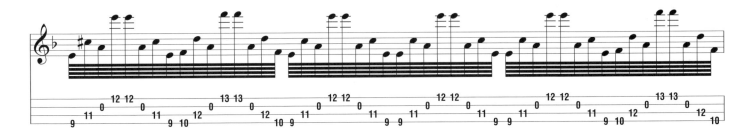

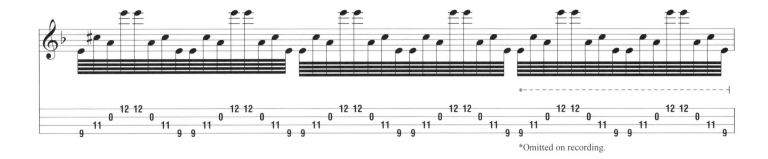

*Omitted on recording.

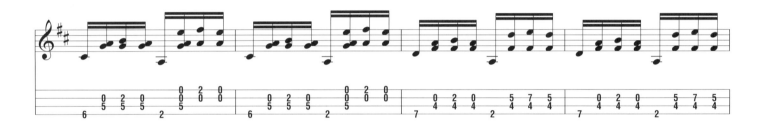

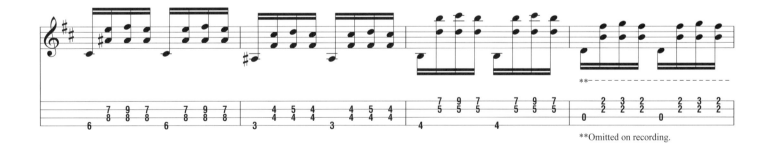

**Omitted on recording.

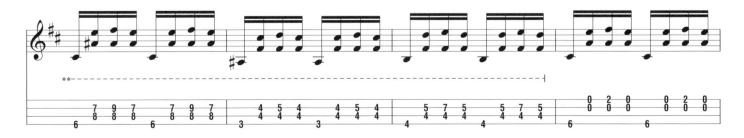

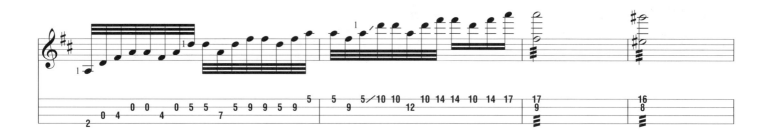

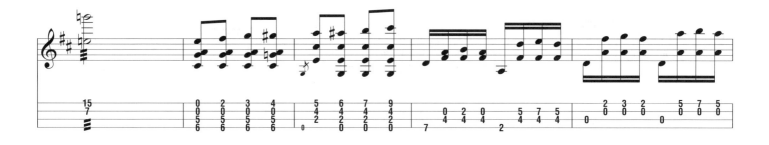

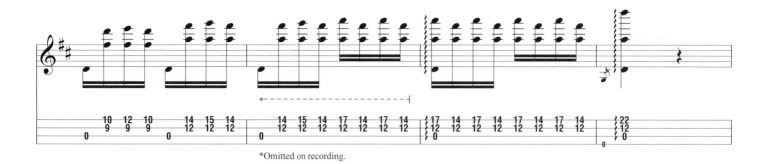

*Omitted on recording.

Vivace

Preludio X

Raffaele Calace
Op. 112

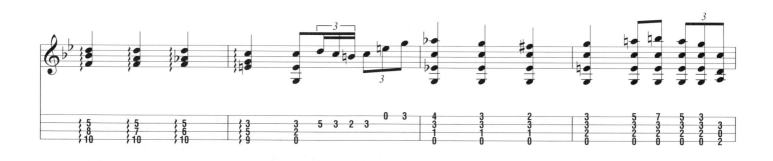

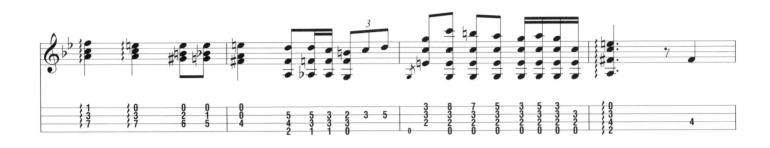

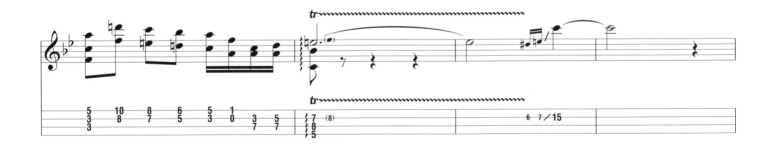

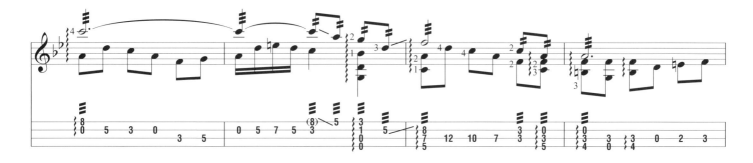

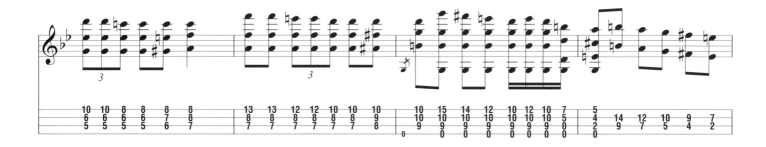

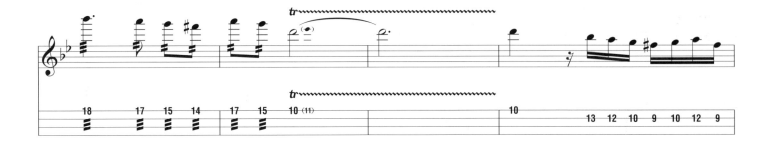

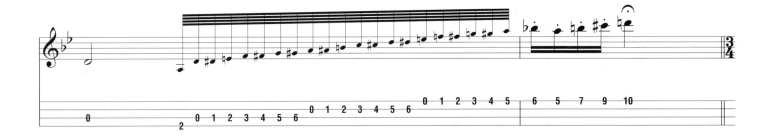

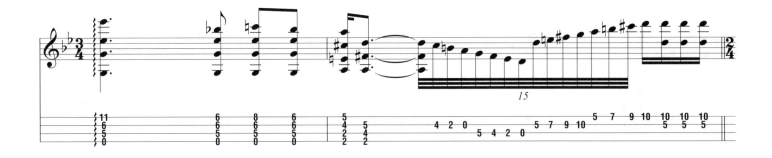

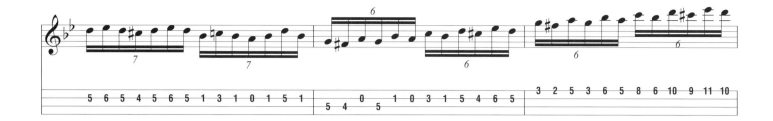

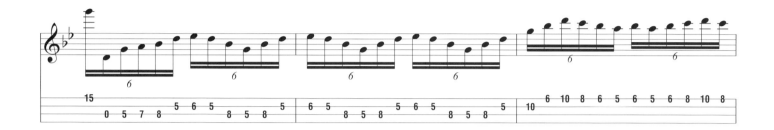

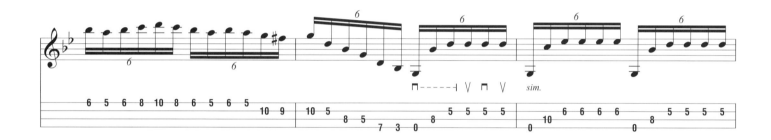

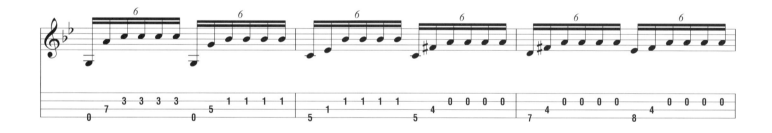

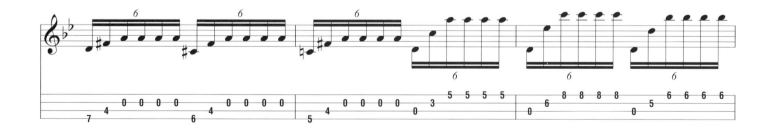

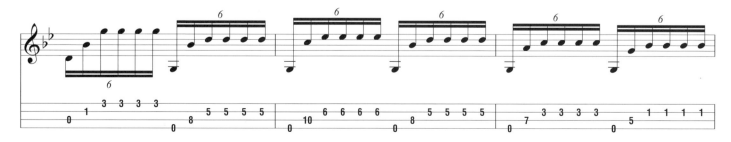

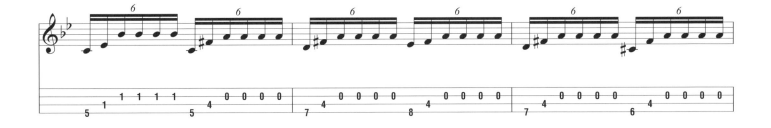

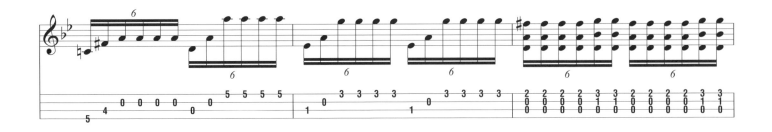

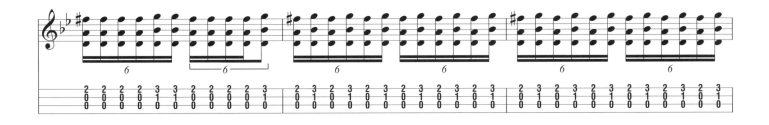

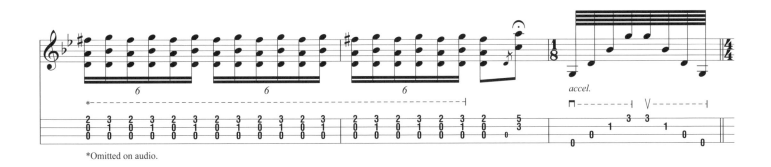

*Omitted on audio.

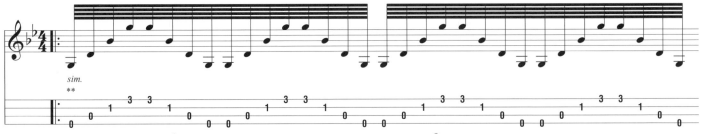

**Original manuscript is in $\frac{3}{4}$ for this repeated section. Delete 2nd beat in each measure to play in $\frac{3}{4}$.

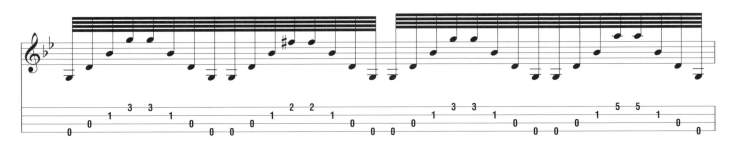

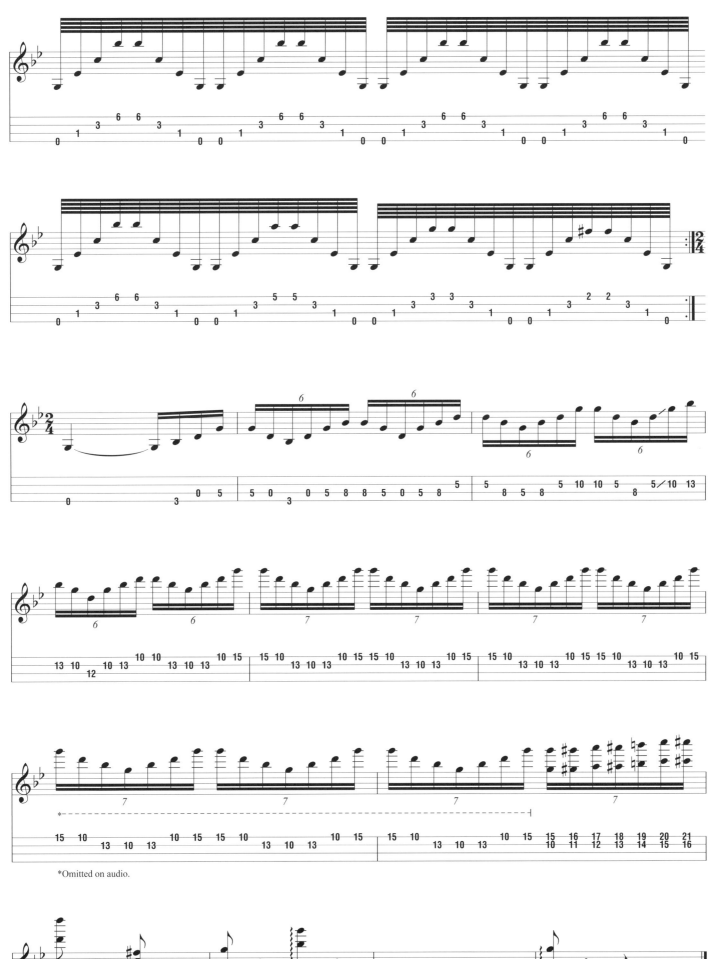

*Omitted on audio.

Golden Rod
(National Flower)
A Barcarolle

Valentine Abt

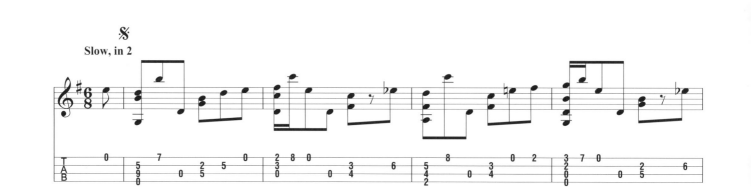

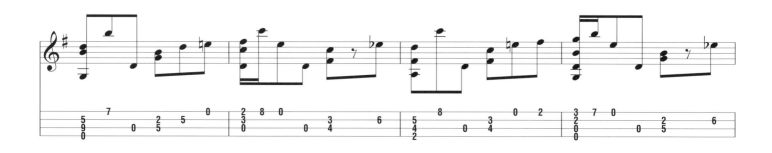

*2nd time, *rit.*

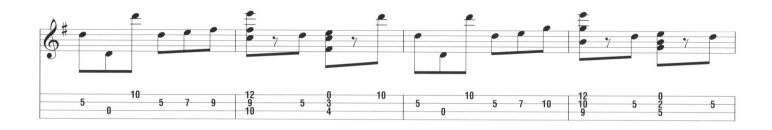

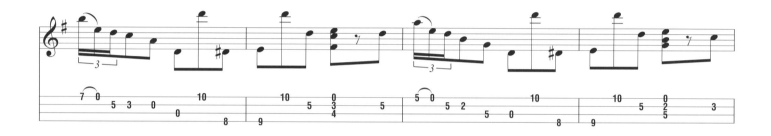

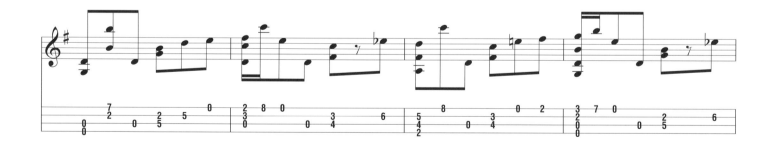

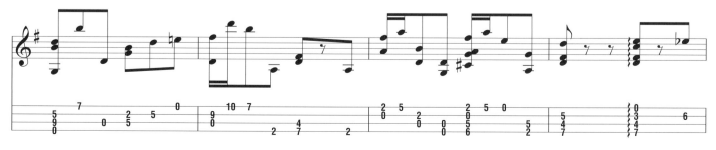

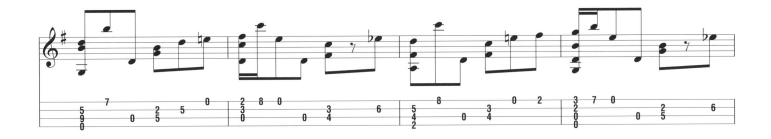

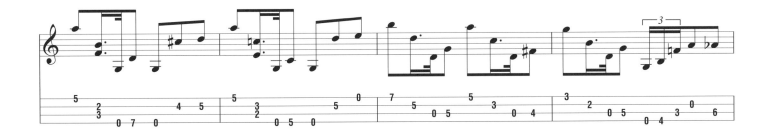

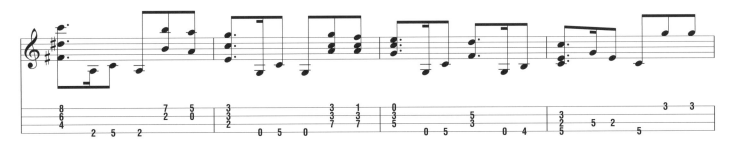

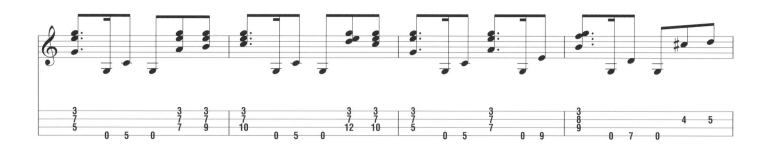

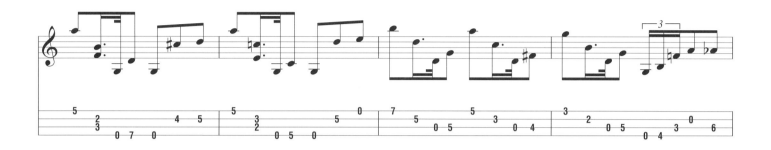

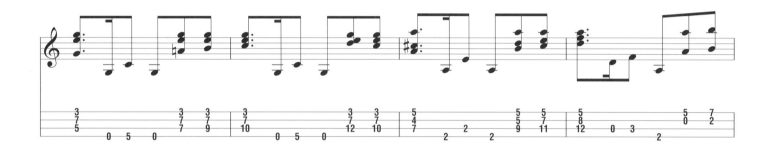

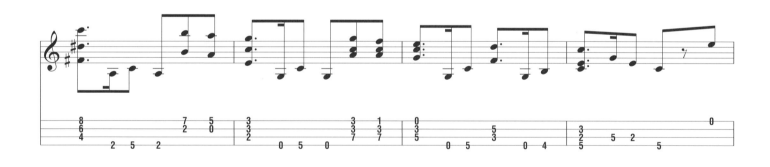

D.S. al Coda

⊕ **Coda**

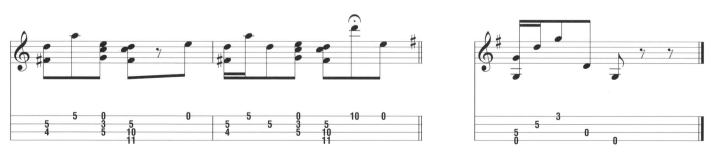

MANDOLIN NOTATION LEGEND

Mandolin music can be notated three different ways: on a *musical staff,* in *tablature,* and in *rhythm slashes.*

RHYTHM SLASHES are written above the staff. Strum chords in the rhythm indicated. Use the chord diagrams found at the top of the first page of the transcription for the appropriate chord voicings.

THE MUSICAL STAFF shows pitches and rhythms and is divided by bar lines into measures. Pitches are named after the first seven letters of the alphabet.

TABLATURE graphically represents the mandolin fretboard. Each of the four horizontal lines represents each of the four courses of strings, and each number represents a fret.

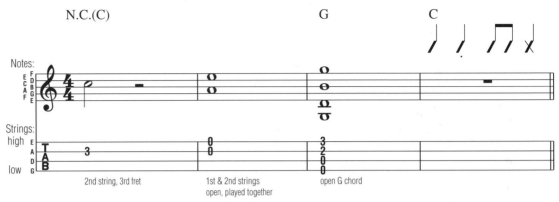

Definitions for Special Mandolin Notation

MUTED STRING(S): Lightly touch a string with the edge of your fret-hand finger while fretting a note on an adjacent string, causing the muted string to be unheard. Muting all of the strings with the fingers of the fret-hand while strumming the strings with the picking hand produces a percussive effect.

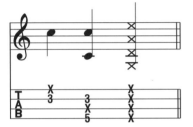

HAMMER-ON: Strike the first (lower) note with one finger, then sound the higher note (on the same string) with another finger by fretting it without picking.

PULL-OFF: Place both fingers on the notes to be sounded. Strike the first note and, without picking, pull the finger off to sound the second (lower) note.

LEGATO SLIDE: Strike the first note and then slide the same fret-hand finger up or down to the second note. The second note is not struck.

SHIFT SLIDE: Same as the legato slide except the second note is struck.

HALF-STEP BEND: Strike the note and bend up ½ step.

GRACE NOTE BEND: Strike the note and immediately bend up as indicated.

TREMOLO PICKING: The note is picked rapidly and continuously.

Additional Musical Definitions

p *(piano)* • Play quietly.

mp *(mezzo-piano)* • Play moderately quiet.

mf *(mezzo-forte)* • Play moderately loud.

f *(forte)* • Play loudly.

cont. rhy. sim. • Continue strumming in similar rhythm.

N.C. *(no chord)* • Don't strum until the next chord symbol. Chord symbols in parentheses reflect implied harmony.

D.S. al Coda • Go back to the sign (𝄋), then play until the measure marked *"To Coda"*, then skip to the section labeled **"Coda."**

D.S.S. al Coda 2 • Go back to the double sign (𝄋𝄋), then play until the measure marked *"To Coda 2"*, then skip to the section labeled **"Coda 2."**

D.S. al Fine • Go back to the sign (𝄋), then play until the label *"Fine."*

(staccato) • Play the note or chord short.

rit. *(ritard)* • Gradually slow down.

(fermata) • Hold the note or chord for an undetermined amount of time.

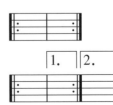

• Repeat measures between signs.

1. 2. • When a repeated section has different endings, play the first ending only the first time and the second ending only the second time.

NOTE: Tablature numbers in parentheses mean:
1. The note is being sustained over a system (note in standard notation is tied), or
2. The note is sustained, but a new articulation (such as a hammer-on, pull-off or slide) begins.